Singing with Joi

There Are Lots of Different Ways to be a Family

Written by : **Joi R. Fisher-Griffin**
Illustrated by : **Sameer Kassar**

© 2021 Joi R. Fisher-Griffin, MindThrive Publishers.

All Rights Reserved.
No part of this book may be reproduced or transmitted in any form or by any means, electronic or mechanical, including photocopying and recording, or by any information storage and retrieval system, without permission in writing from author and publisher.

Printed in the United States of America
2021 First Edition

Subject Index:
Fisher-Griffin, Joi R.
Title: Singing with Joi: There Are Lots of Different Ways to be a Family
1. Adoption 2. Foster Care 3. Education

Paperback ISBN: 978-1-733-6314-2-6
Library of Congress Control Number: 2021913461

www.findingjoi.us
MindThrive Publishers L.L.C.
The Belong Project: An Adoption Awareness Campaign
www.thebelongproject.us

Dedication

This book is dedicated to the entire New Jersey Coalition for Adoption Reform and Education (NJCARE) Legislative Team; Pam Hasegawa, Judy Foster, William Mild, Carol Barbieri, Tom McGee, Michele Fortier, Pete Franklin, Aletia Morgan. Alyce Jenkins, Jane Nast, Maryann Pisani, Randie Zimmerman, Deborah Hurley, Peggi Sturmfels, Bob Hafetz, Mary Mild, Betsy Forrest, and Susan Merkel. Thank you for the sacrifices made over 34 years to affect change in our state. And I cannot forget Marty Frumpkin and David Petruzziello who currently lead our Morristown Support Group. Thank you for hosting a supportive and welcoming support group. Thank you ALL for encouraging me to take a leap of faith and speak out in my circles of influence.

My life is forever changed.

"What about your real mom and dad?" sneered Michael in the corridor.

"We don't say 'real.' We say birth parents and adoptive parents," Joi snapped.

"Yes," said the counselor. "We are all raised in different ways. Michael, you stay with your cousins in the summers, right?"

Michael pouted. "I guess."

The counselor nodded. "Now, are you two going to sign up for the talent show? We are allowing parent-child teams this year!"

Joi excitedly signed her and her dad's name on the sheet. Michael saw.

"Your dad? Ha, he's so old," Michael said. "No one will know he's your parent."

"Well, you are wrong," Joi said. "We are going to *ace* those auditions*!*"

Then, it was the evening of the auditions.

The school hall was filled with other families.

Joi looked around at them.

There were Nick and his mom with the exact same hair.

Anna and her dad, both with the same blue eyes and glasses.

Dante and his grandpa with the same winning smile.

Joi and her dad were both tall but looked nothing like each other. She felt nervous and ran over to the refreshment table.

"Hey!" said the teenager behind the stall. "You're the only one performing by yourself."

"No! I'm with my dad…" Joi pointed.

"Oh!" the teenager said. "Right, yeah, you're adopted, aren't you?" she leaned in. "Like, I've always wondered, don't adopted kids cost a lot…?"

Joi grabbed two cups and hurried off.

The older girl hadn't meant to be mean, but Joi was scared it was true.

But Joi's eyes were filled with tears as she ran up to Dad. Her foot slipped!

"Ow! I'm sorry, Joi. I don't think I'll be able to play the keyboard anymore."

"Next up to audition: Joi and her dad!" said Mr. Smith.

Joi looked up. To her horror, everyone was looking their way.

"Some of you have been raised by your grandparents." Joi said when she finished. "Some of you have two dads, some of you have a mom and dad, and some of you have just your mom."

"There are lots of different ways to be a family," Joi continued. "And my family happens to represent one of those differences. Yes, I was legally allowed to be adopted by people who are not my biological parents. That simply

Off stage, the other kids came up to Joi.

"Awesome song!" Anna said. "I guess even in natural born families, not all family members look similar."

"All of our families look different. The talent show showed us there is love in each one," Joi said. "Let's respect our differences!"

They all joined in as Joi sang:

Don't be ashamed, be proud. Make your voice heard, right now. Share your story, you're unique. You'll find joy, and you'll find peace. The truth could never be wrong. Just know that you belong. You belong, you belong. You belong, you belong It's OK to be different. Family loves never ending.

Vocabulary List

Adopt — to legally take the responsibility of a child or adult as their parent. To begin by choice into a legal relationship as a parent or a child or adult.

Adopted — when a child or adult legally becomes part of a family

Adoptee — the child or adult who is adopted

Adoption — the process or act of adopting, taking the legal responsibilities as a parent of a child or adult that is not their biological child

Adoptive/Adopted Parent — one who becomes a parent through the process of adoption.

Birth/Bio Parent — the biological parents whose DNA matches the child. The mother who gave birth to the child and the father who by birth is the male parent of the child.

Foster Parent — a person or people who care for a child who is not their biological child. They take the child into their home for a period of time.

Relinquished — when a birth parent places a child for adoption

Temporary — only lasts for a period of time; it is not permanent

About the Author

Author and entrepreneur Joi R. Fisher-Griffin is an experienced educator, a passionate adoption advocate and patron of the arts. After going through her own struggles as an adoptee, Joi wrote her memoir, Finding Joi: A True Story of Faith, Family, and Love, which debuted in 2019. She shared her story so that she could help  others who sit in silence about their struggles, and she continues to find ways to be open about adoption, not only with adults but to start the conversation with young people, too. Joi established The Belong Project: An Adoption Awareness Campaign as her signature talk to help normalize conversations around adoption and she serves as the Adult Adoptee & Survivor Team Coordinator with Miriam's Heart organization in New Jersey.

www.findingjoi.us

Check out the link to lyric video on the website for the song 'You Belong'

www.ingramcontent.com/pod-product-compliance
Lightning Source LLC
LaVergne TN
LVHW071030070426
835507LV00002B/93